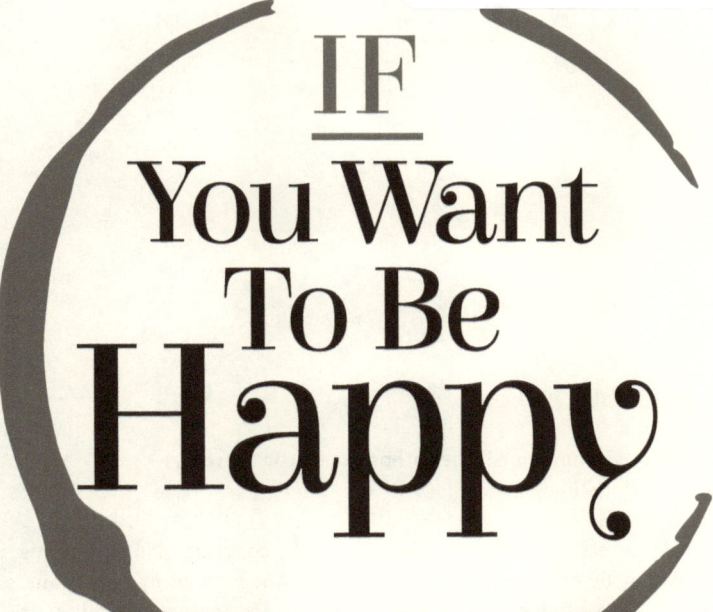

IF
You Want
To Be
Happy

AN EASY-TO-READ GUIDE ON HOW
TO CREATE YOUR HAPPINESS...
IF YOU WANT IT!

JULIE FIDALGO

Dedicated to my mom and dad.
Thank you for your unconditional
love and support.

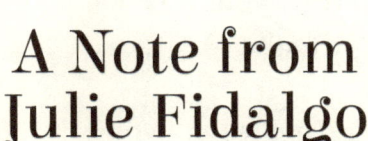

A Note from Julie Fidalgo

I believe that everyone *wishes* they could be happy, but what most people don't realize is that it's up to them to *create* their own happiness.

People think that happiness comes from somewhere, something, or someone, but the truth is that happiness comes from within *you*.

It's a difficult idea to swallow, because once you know it's in your hands, you are now responsible for your own happiness. And most people would rather blame it on external factors than take accountability.

Happiness is a choice. Yes, life has its ups and downs, but it's important to have the *intention* to be happy. Every day. Being happy doesn't mean you don't have problems; it just means you are able to work through them with a positive mindset.

Let's be real—life isn't easy, and happiness isn't something that is constant. But to know that it is up to you to create your own happiness is the first step to a happy life.

In these pages, I share with you a list I have formed of simple concepts that have allowed me to create my own happiness. Each concept introduced is in its most basic form.

This guide is easy to read, simple to understand, and possible to apply. The tools are straightforward, but putting them to work requires patience, a burning desire to change, and the courage to overcome challenges.

If you want to be happy... you *really* have to want it!

I am dedicated to your happiness. Are you?

~Julie Fidalgo

Tips on how to read this book

- If possible, read this book in its entirety in one sitting before filling anything out.

- Go back and read it a second time and fill in the spaces provided.

- Use this book as a manual and refer back to it when needed.

- Be sure to use the space provided to write out the answers to the questions. This will help you reflect on the question at hand and provide a thought you had never considered before.

- Carry it with you in your bag or keep it in the car for when inspiration (or crisis) hits.

- Read a few concepts at a time before bed so it can sink into your subconscious mind.

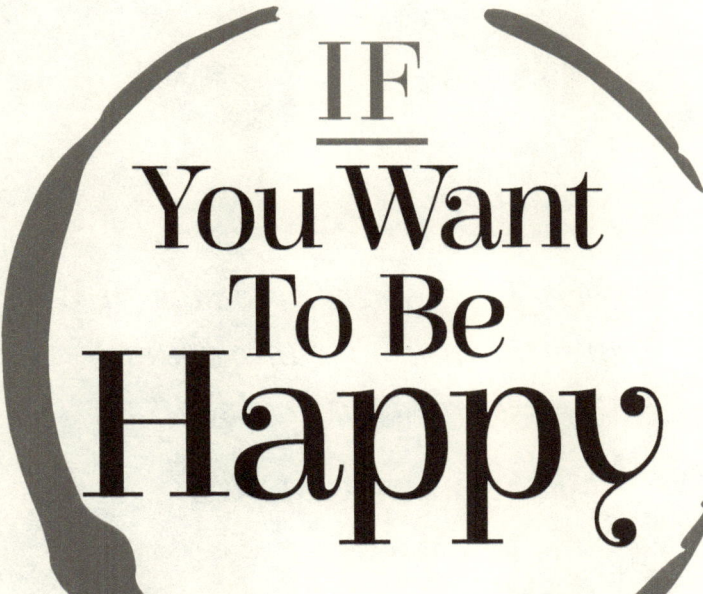

IF
You Want To Be
To Be
Happy

"Very little is needed to make a happy life; it is all within yourself, in your way of thinking."

-MARCUS AURELIUS

What does happiness look like to you? Describe it here:

_____

_____

_____

_____

_____

_____

_____

_____

_____

_____

_____

_____

_____

_____

_____

_____

_____

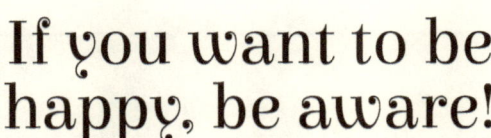

If you want to be happy, be aware!

The definition of awareness is having the knowledge or perception of a situation or fact. The definition of self-awareness is the conscious knowledge of one's own character, feelings, motives, and desires.

When we are self-aware, we see ourselves clearly; we know who we are, we know what we want, and we know what it takes to get there. People who are self-aware tend to have more confidence. Having more confidence can lead to more happiness.

When we are self-aware, we tend to make better decisions and have better relationships. This affects our happiness.

How to be (more) aware:

Know yourself: Self-awareness is the foundation of authenticity. Know your values, strengths, and weaknesses.

Be truthful (with yourself and others) and always follow your intuition.

Consider how your actions affect yourself and others.

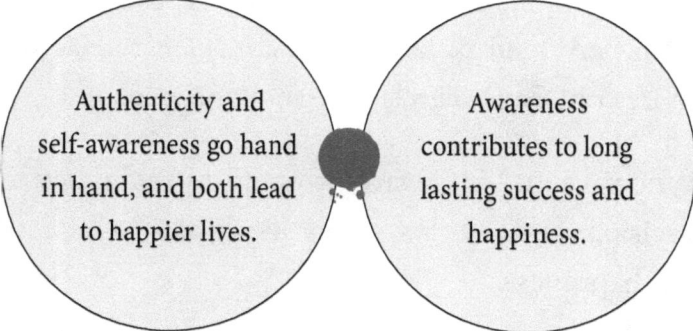

Authenticity and self-awareness go hand in hand, and both lead to happier lives.

Awareness contributes to long lasting success and happiness.

JULIE FIDALGO

What are your values? What do you believe with all your heart?

_____

_____

_____

_____

_____

_____

_____

_____

_____

_____

_____

_____

_____

_____

_____

_____

_____

_____

_____

"Happiness is a choice that requires self–AWARENESS and a determination to live in the present moment."

-UNKNOWN

If you want to be happy, take good care of your brain!

Your brain is very special. It is the command center of your body and controls everything you feel, think, and do.

The brain is like a computer—it can learn to do new things. But like a computer, it cannot know if what it is being taught is good or bad. You must be careful when learning new habits or thought patterns. You should try and only teach your brain good things.

The brain loves to learn, and the more you use it, the more it expands. How you use your brain will determine your life; therefore, taking good care of your brain is essential for a happy life.

How to take good care of your brain:

Get good sleep. Without proper sleep, the brain is unable to function efficiently.

Eat a healthy diet. Some of the best foods for your brain include avocados, blueberries, dark chocolate, green leafy vegetables, turmeric, and eggs. And don't forget to drink water!

Always keep learning! Read books, take a class, engage in new experiences, learn a new language, or learn how to play an instrument.

The human brain is only fully developed at age twenty-five.

Serotonin in the brain regulates your mood. It creates a feeling of happiness.

JULIE FIDALGO

What do you do to take care of your brain?

_____

_____

_____

_____

_____

_____

_____

_____

_____

_____

_____

_____

_____

_____

_____

"Your BRAIN works just like a computer, so make sure you're the only one programming it."

-THE MINDS JOURNAL

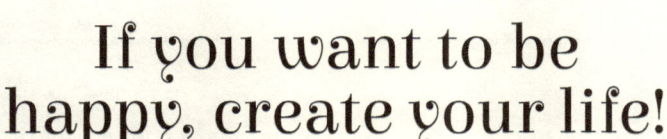

If you want to be happy, create your life!

You have the power to create your life, but first you have to decide what you want your life to look like.

You can't create anything without first having a vision and a plan. Creating your life is the same. Start thinking about the life you want, and every day, take positive steps toward achieving that life. You may not yet know *how* to do it, but the how will show itself.

Action brings clarity, motivation, and results. Keep moving forward and never stop. Remember that anything is possible. Nothing is impossible.

How to create your life:

Find out your purpose—what would you like to spend your days doing?

Create a vision board*. Add as much detail as possible and keep changing it as the things you want change.

Make a list of small steps you can take today toward the life you want. For instance, if you want to be healthier, your first step could be taking daily walks.

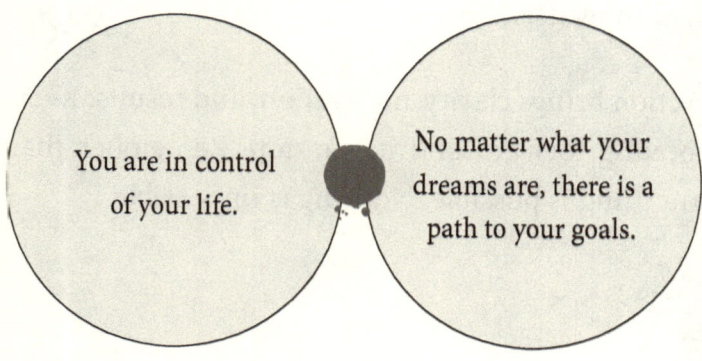

You are in control of your life.

No matter what your dreams are, there is a path to your goals.

JULIE FIDALGO

What do you want your life to look like?

_____

_____

_____

_____

_____

_____

_____

_____

_____

_____

_____

_____

_____

_____

_____

_____

_____

"Life isn't about finding yourself; life is about CREATING yourself."

-GEORGE BERNARD SHAW

If you want to be happy, get good at making decisions!

Decisions are important for your life to move forward. Of course, there are good decisions and there are bad ones. The good ones will lead you in the right direction and the bad ones will teach you lessons.

Life is about the choices we make; essentially, the decisions in life's moments. Every decision has repercussions. Make sure your decisions are thought through before committing to them.

If you don't like the direction your life is headed due to bad decisions, make the decision to change it, and make decisions that will help you get to where you want to be.

How to get good at making decisions:

Gather as much information as possible and evaluate the situation.

Consider the options of the decision; take your time, brainstorm, and seek guidance.

Trusting your intuition is extremely important when it comes to decision making. Do not ignore that little voice that speaks to you.

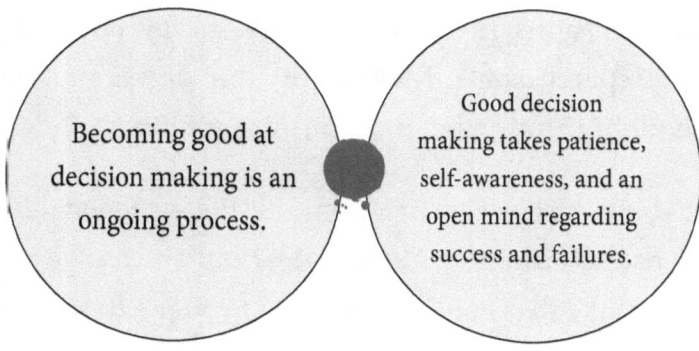

Becoming good at decision making is an ongoing process.

Good decision making takes patience, self-awareness, and an open mind regarding success and failures.

Can you think of a choice or decision you made in the past that you are proud of? How did it make you feel? Write about it here.

_____

_____

_____

_____

_____

_____

_____

_____

_____

_____

_____

_____

_____

_____

_____

"The quality of your DECISION making will determine the quality of your life."

-RAY DALIO

If you want to be happy, change your energy!

Energy is everywhere. Everything is energy. It's something you can't see but you can feel. Even our thoughts and emotions have energy. This is why it's important to always think and *feel* positive.

Positivity keeps our energy at a good level. We need to spend as much time as possible being around positive people and doing what we love so we *feel* good.

When you change your energy, you change your life. Your energy, when vibrating high, attracts people with the same energy. Positive people attract other positive people, just as positive experiences also attract other positive experiences.

How to change your energy:

Spend time in nature. Get your body moving. Listen to upbeat music.

Think of your future self and who you want to be. Have the intention to be that person and immerse in the feelings of what it would be like to live in that future.

When you begin to have a negative thought, take a deep breath and change it to a positive thought. It becomes easier with practice.

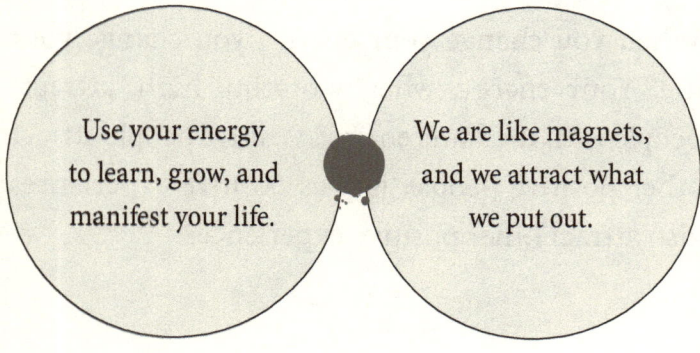

Use your energy to learn, grow, and manifest your life.

We are like magnets, and we attract what we put out.

Your energy levels may be affected by where you are. Write about how you feel in different places and discover where your energy level is the highest.

_____

_____

_____

_____

_____

_____

_____

_____

_____

_____

_____

_____

_____

_____

"Everything is ENERGY, and that's all there is to it. Match the frequency of the reality you want, and you cannot help but get that reality. It can be no other way. This is not philosophy. This is physics."

-ALBERT EINSTEIN

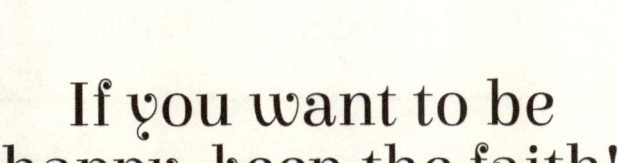

If you want to be happy, keep the faith!

Faith is trusting that everything will work out. Sometimes it might not seem that way, but never lose faith in yourself and your dreams.

Having faith will help you get what you want. Staying optimistic and trusting that everything will work out at the right time is necessary to be happy.

Faith helps you stop agonizing over the past and worrying about the future. Trust that the future and the unknown are filled with positive experiences. Faith allows you to trust that everything will be okay.

How to keep the faith:

Keep your dreams alive and believe they are possible, even if people tell you otherwise.

Find ways to stay inspired, even when things are difficult. When things get tough, keep the faith.

When challenges arise, trust in yourself; obstacles are usually there for us to prove how much we want it. Believe that it's going to happen when the time is right.

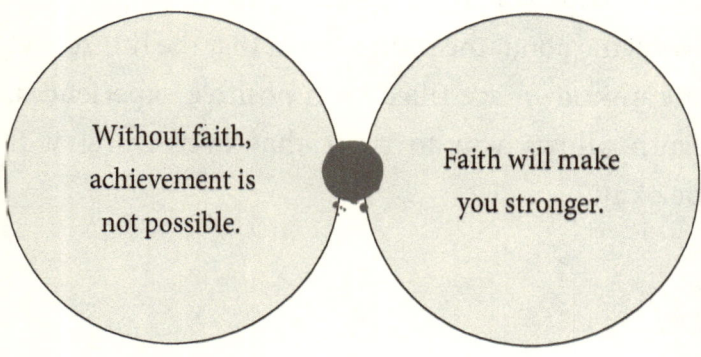

Without faith, achievement is not possible.

Faith will make you stronger.

JULIE FIDALGO

Often, things don't happen like you planned, and afterward you might realize it was actually a good thing. Do you remember this ever happening to you? Write about it.

_____

_____

_____

_____

_____

_____

_____

_____

_____

_____

_____

_____

_____

_____

"Take the first step in FAITH. You don't have to see the whole staircase. Just take the first step."

-DR. MARTIN LUTHER KING, JR.

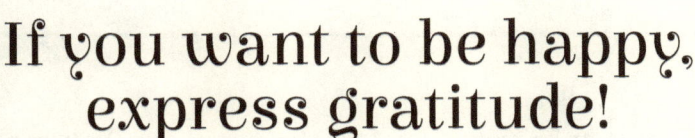

If you want to be happy, express gratitude!

To express gratitude is to be thankful. You should always be grateful for what you receive, no matter how small. The more grateful you are, the more life will give you.

Sometimes it can be difficult to be grateful, but it's a lot easier when you focus on what you *do* have rather than what you don't.

The happiest people don't necessarily have the best of everything, they just make the best of what they have!

The more grateful you are the more positive you feel and the more joy can enter your life. Being grateful also makes the people around you feel happier, so everyone wins!

How to express gratitude:

Give thanks every day for what you have. You can do this in simple ways, like saying thank you and *feeling* genuine gratitude.

Don't be jealous of others. Everyone is on their own journey, and comparing yourself to others only hurts you.

Help others who are less fortunate.

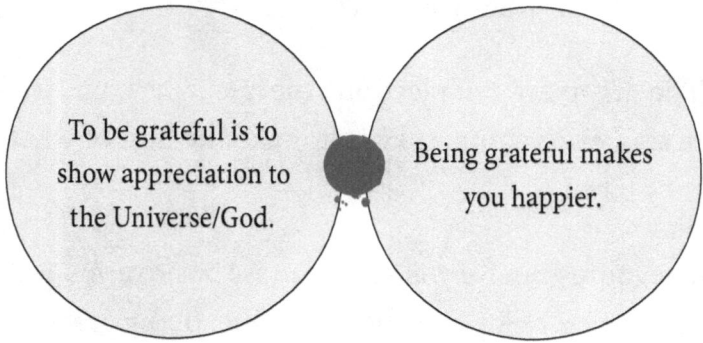

To be grateful is to show appreciation to the Universe/God.

Being grateful makes you happier.

What are you grateful for? Write it down.

_____

_____

_____

_____

_____

_____

_____

_____

_____

_____

_____

_____

_____

_____

_____

"Your GRATITUDE is magnetic, and the more GRATITUDE you have, the more abundance you magnetize."

-RHONDA BYRNE

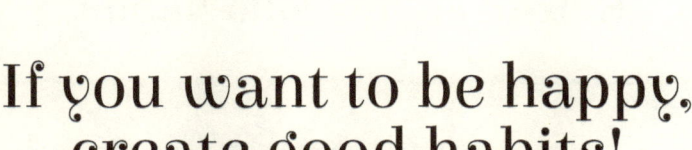

If you want to be happy, create good habits!

We all have habits, but not all our habits are good. Your life is a sum of all of your habits, the good, the bad, and the ugly!

Good habits can make your life better and can make achieving your goals a lot easier. Bad habits stop you from getting what you want out of life.

Work toward creating and building good habits and getting rid of the bad ones. Having a plan or a system in place helps you stay on track when breaking bad habits and creating good ones. It may be difficult in the beginning; you have to really want it.

How to create good habits:

Become aware of your bad habits and take steps every day to replace the bad habits with good choices.

Decide and plan on how to create and stick to positive habits.

Celebrate the wins, even if they are small.

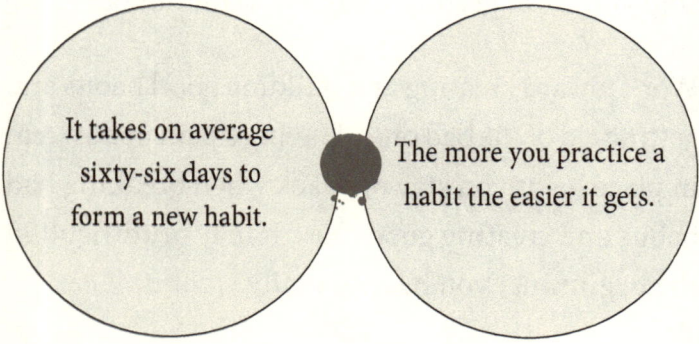

It takes on average sixty-six days to form a new habit.

The more you practice a habit the easier it gets.

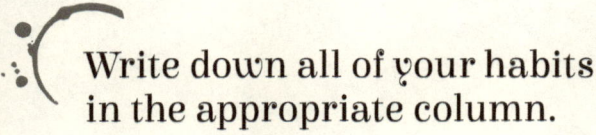

Write down all of your habits
in the appropriate column.

Good habits:

_____

_____

_____

_____

_____

_____

Bad habits:

_____

_____

_____

_____

_____

_____

"People do not decide their futures, they decide their HABITS and their HABITS decide their futures."

-F.M ALEXANDER

If you want to be happy, use your imagination!

Every new discovery started with an idea created in someone's imagination. Einstein said, "Imagination is more important than knowledge. Knowledge is limited. Imagination encircles the world."

If you can imagine it, you can be, do, or have anything. Imagination allows you to "see" the future outcomes of your decisions. Anything is possible in your imagination. Pablo Picasso said, "Everything you can imagine is real."

By imagining something, you can come up with great new ideas. Your imagination is a safe space to try new things or see the life you are working toward.

How to use your imagination:

Daydream. Imagine scenarios and situations that you want to attract into your life. Daydreaming should bring in positive feelings.

Try new things. Bring your inner child back into your life and explore, stay curious, and play!

Spend some time alone without any distractions and allow your mind to flow without any judgments.

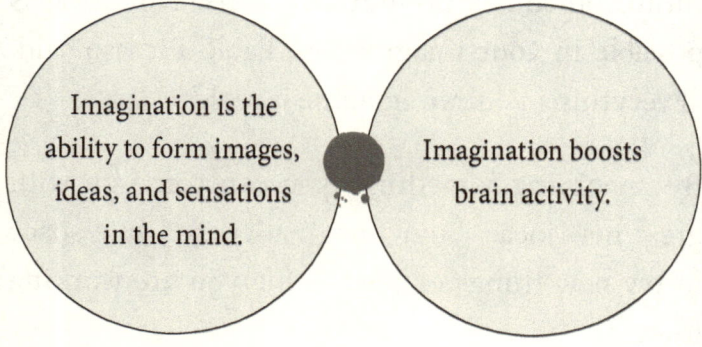

Imagination is the ability to form images, ideas, and sensations in the mind.

Imagination boosts brain activity.

JULIE FIDALGO

How do you use your imagination?
What specific things can you do
to expand your imagination?

_____

_____

_____

_____

_____

_____

_____

_____

_____

_____

_____

_____

_____

_____

_____

_____

_____

"IMAGINATION is everything. It is the preview to life's coming attractions."

-ALBERT EINSTEIN

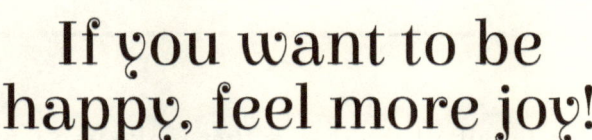

If you want to be happy, feel more joy!

The more joy you feel, the happier you will be. To feel joy is to feel good. Although this might seem impossible on some days, it will become easier if you try.

Finding joy doesn't have to be a huge mission; joy can be found in the simplest things. A smile from someone. A beautiful flower. The smell of pancakes!

Try to feel joy every day, whether that's taking a walk or reading a book. Whenever you feel joy, take notice of it and how it makes you feel. Try to make the feeling last. And then repeat.

How to feel more joy:

Make a list of all the things that make you happy, then do more of that.

Connect with people you love and who make you feel good. Spend more time with people who bring you joy.

Do something every day that brings you joy, and find joy in the little things in life.

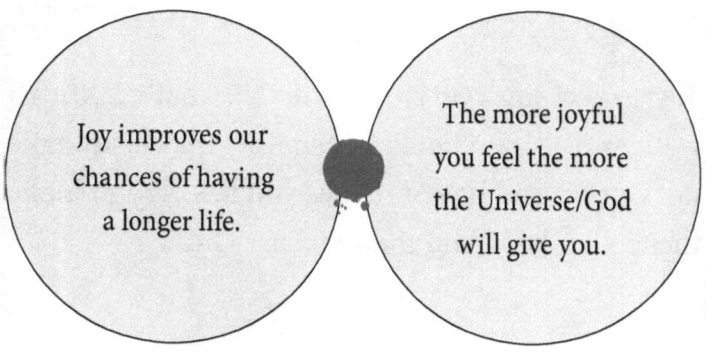

Joy improves our chances of having a longer life.

The more joyful you feel the more the Universe/God will give you.

Make a list of everything that brings you joy.

_____

_____

_____

_____

_____

_____

_____

_____

_____

_____

_____

_____

_____

_____

_____

_____

_____

"JOY does not simply happen to us. We have to choose JOY and keep choosing it every day."

–HENRI J.M. NOUMEN

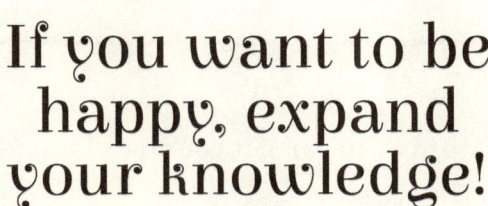

If you want to be happy, expand your knowledge!

Knowledge is power, but only when knowledge is put to work. Knowledge by itself won't get you far, but it provides opportunity if you use it correctly.

It is what you do with knowledge that makes all the difference. Be sure the knowledge you gain is of good quality and that you can use it to make the world a better place.

Expand your mind. Keep learning. No knowledge is ever for nothing. Knowledge is growth, and growth is life. Stay curious!

How to expand your knowledge:

Read anything you can get your hands on. Reading expands your mind.

Don't be afraid to ask questions. When you don't know something, ask! You will leave the situation with more knowledge.

Say yes to new experiences. We learn and attain knowledge by doing; therefore, we should continuously try new things.

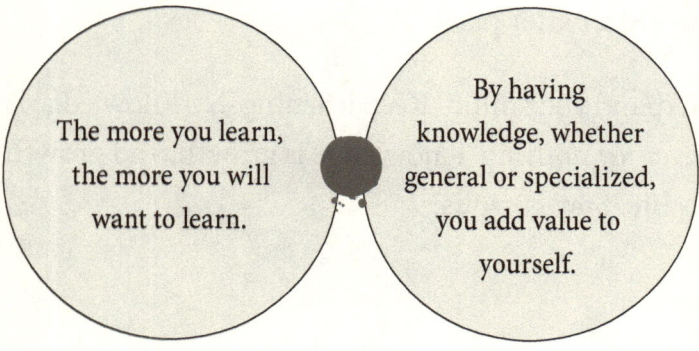

The more you learn, the more you will want to learn.

By having knowledge, whether general or specialized, you add value to yourself.

What three topics would you like to learn about and why?

_____

_____

_____

_____

_____

_____

_____

_____

_____

_____

_____

_____

_____

_____

_____

_____

"Today KNOWLEDGE has power. It controls access to opportunity and advancement."

-PETER DRUCKER

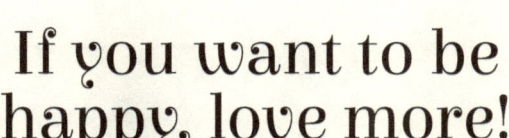

If you want to be happy, love more!

Loving others is important, but the most important love is to love yourself. Self-love means taking good care of mind, body, and soul and feeling good about yourself.

Everyone has parts of themselves that they don't like, but loving yourself means you have an appreciation for yourself and everything you've been through. Loving yourself is a healthy kind of love. Life isn't easy, but you've made it this far.

Love yourself and love others. Treat yourself with respect and respect others. Appreciate yourself and appreciate others.

How to love more:

Make a list of all your positive qualities and focus on them.

Be kind to yourself. Learn from your past mistakes and forgive yourself.

Take care of your mind, body, and soul. Your future self will thank you for it.

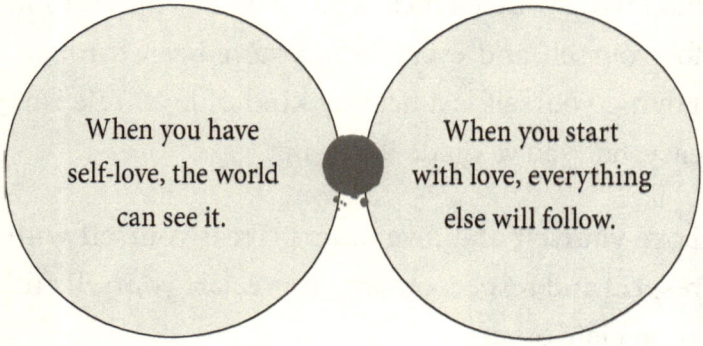

When you have self-love, the world can see it.

When you start with love, everything else will follow.

What do you love about yourself?

"LOVE yourself first, and everything else falls into line. You really have to LOVE yourself to get anything done in this world."

-LUCILLE BALL

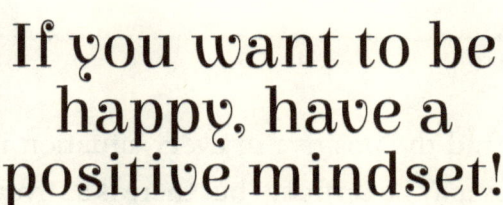

If you want to be happy, have a positive mindset!

If you want to be happy, you have to have a positive mindset. This will help lead you toward happiness.

Mindset is how your brain sees yourself and the world around you. Mindset helps you look at problems in specific ways. For instance, a positive mindset will help you look at your issues positively.

Having a positive mindset is not always easy, but the more you practice it, the easier it will become.

How to have a positive mindset:

Try to find the positive in every situation in your life. This may be difficult, but there is a silver lining to everything.

Don't let failure discourage you or affect your mood. Tell yourself that you'll try again next time.

Praise yourself when you know you've done well and keep on keeping on.

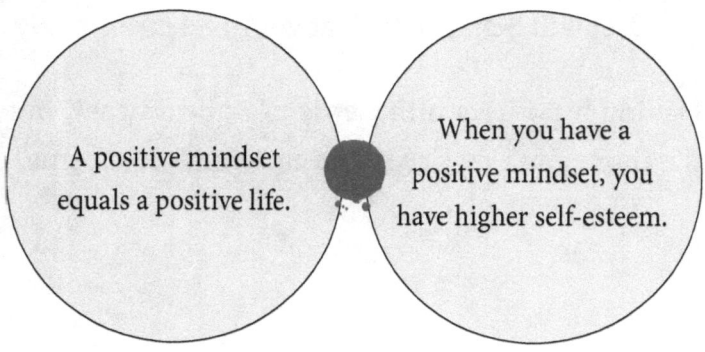

A positive mindset equals a positive life.

When you have a positive mindset, you have higher self-esteem.

Can you think of a situation
when something bad happened
and try to find the good in
it? Write about it here.

_____

_____

_____

_____

_____

_____

_____

_____

_____

_____

_____

_____

_____

_____

_____

*"Your life is as good as
your MINDSET."*

-ANONYMOUS

If you want to be happy, live in the now!

Living in the now will make you happier. Spending time thinking about the past won't change the past. Spending time worrying about the future won't do you any good.

Being present in the now is important, and anxious feelings tend to disappear when you live in the present moment. Everything happens when it's supposed to happen. Trust the timing of occurrences in life.

Now is the only time that things can get done. Anything done now will help change tomorrow. Connect to the now, and you'll discover that living in the present moment is powerful.

How to live in the now:

Focus on the moment and be mindful of your actions.

Meditate* daily and pay attention to the small things around you. Reduce distractions.

Avoid worrying about the future. This will only bring you anxiety and distract you from living in the present moment.

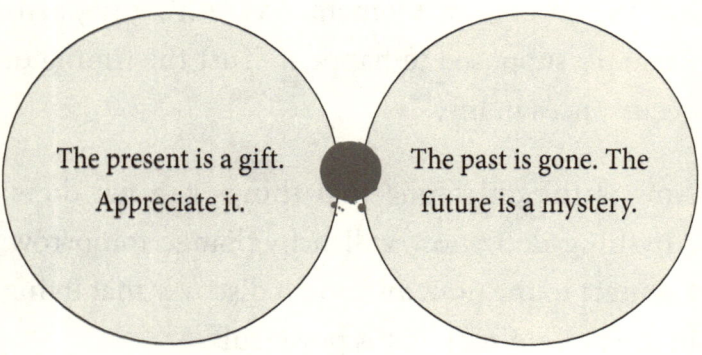

The present is a gift. Appreciate it.

The past is gone. The future is a mystery.

What can you do to help yourself focus on the moment?

"Realize deeply that the present is all you have. Make the NOW the primary focus of your life."

-AMIT RAY

If you want to be happy, create opportunities!

Creating your own opportunities will bring you happiness. It is something that everyone can do. There are opportunities all around you; all you have to do is look for them.

If you want something, don't be afraid to ask. A failed opportunity can bring about a new and better one. Remember that action cures fear.

If you don't see an opportunity, create your own. Knowing who you are and what you bring to the table, having confidence, and keeping an open mind are tools which will help you create new opportunities.

How to create opportunities:

Try new things and don't be discouraged when things don't work out as planned. Even failure is an opportunity to learn and grow.

Don't be afraid to do things on your own. Don't always depend on other people if you don't have to.

If you want something, ask for it and be creative when looking to create new opportunities.

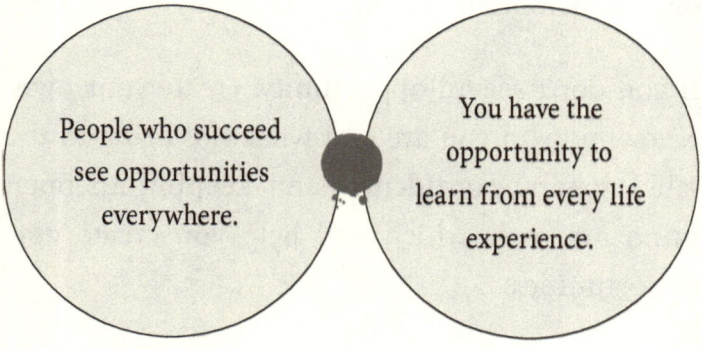

People who succeed see opportunities everywhere.

You have the opportunity to learn from every life experience.

Make a list of new things that you can try. How does it make you feel when you try something new?

_____

_____

_____

_____

_____

_____

_____

_____

_____

_____

_____

_____

_____

_____

_____

_____

_____

_____

"If OPPORTUNITY doesn't knock, build a door."

-MILTON BERLE

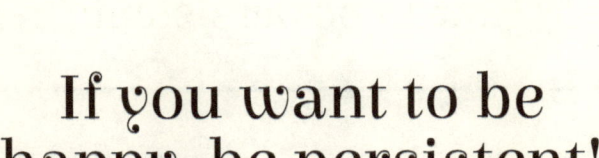

If you want to be happy, be persistent!

If you want something, and that something is going to make you happy, you *have* to be persistent.

Persistence is when you keep going even when you are faced with challenges. Persistence means not giving up, even if you feel frustrated and defeated.

Very few people succeed the first time they try something new. It is persistence that leads to success. Winners never quit and quitters never win. Keep going, be persistent, and eventually, you will succeed.

How to be persistent:

Keep going when things get tough. If the task at hand seems difficult, break it into smaller bites.

Learn how to stay calm when faced with frustration. Take responsibility for your failures and your achievements.

Have a goal and plan and work toward it. Encourage and believe in yourself and your dreams.

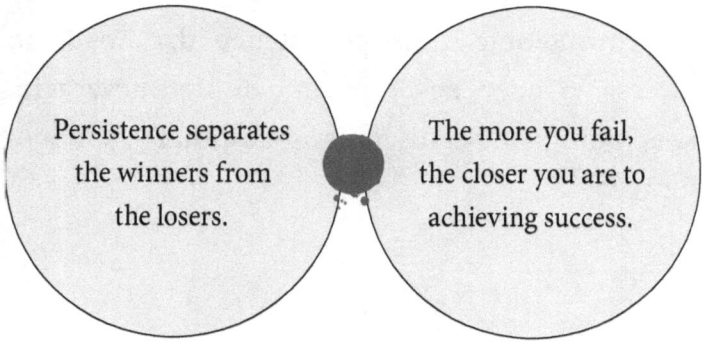

Persistence separates the winners from the losers.

The more you fail, the closer you are to achieving success.

JULIE FIDALGO

What is one thing you want so badly you are willing to keep going until you succeed?

_____

_____

_____

_____

_____

_____

_____

_____

_____

_____

_____

_____

_____

_____

"PERSISTANCE guarantees that results are inevitable."

–PARAMAHANSA YOGANANDA

If you want to be happy, be a person of quality!

A person of quality is a person who is honest and has integrity and self-awareness. He or she is always striving to be better through personal growth and improvement.

When you know that you are striving to be the best version of yourself, this can lead to higher levels of satisfaction. You will likely be satisfied with your choices and actions, and this leads to overall happiness.

Being a person of quality will also attract other people of quality into your life. It can also make a huge difference in the world. When you lead with positive qualities, you impact the lives of those around you.

How to be a person of quality:

Define your values. What do you believe in? What kind of person do you want to be?

Be reliable. Keep your promises and commitments to yourself and to others.

Take responsibility. Learn from your mistakes and acknowledge them. Do better next time.

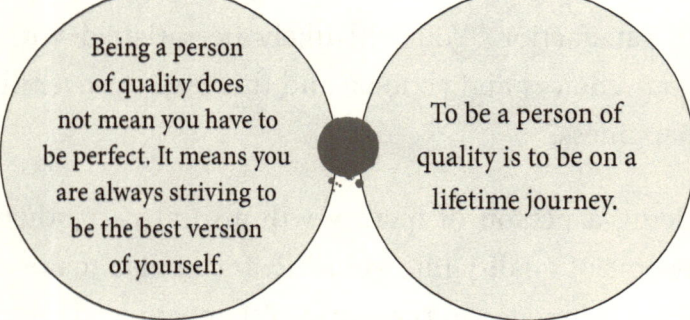

Being a person of quality does not mean you have to be perfect. It means you are always striving to be the best version of yourself.

To be a person of quality is to be on a lifetime journey.

What does being a person of quality mean to you?

_____

_____

_____

_____

_____

_____

_____

_____

_____

_____

_____

_____

_____

_____

_____

_____

_____

"The key to keeping QUALITY people around you is to become a person of QUALITY yourself."

-MAC DUKE

If you want to be happy, maintain healthy relationships!

Good relationships keep us happier and healthier. When we have people who truly care about us, it provides a strong support system.

Having healthy relationships gives us a sense of community and belonging, and this can be beneficial for our personal growth and resilience.

When we have positive interactions with people we have good relationships with, it brings on positive emotions. Those positive emotions lead to more happiness.

How to maintain healthy relationships:

Avoid people and relationships that bring out the worst in you. Create boundaries with people who bring you down.

Cultivate your healthy relationships by giving them your time, attention, and support.

Surround yourself with people who truly care about you, want the best for you, and accept you for who you are.

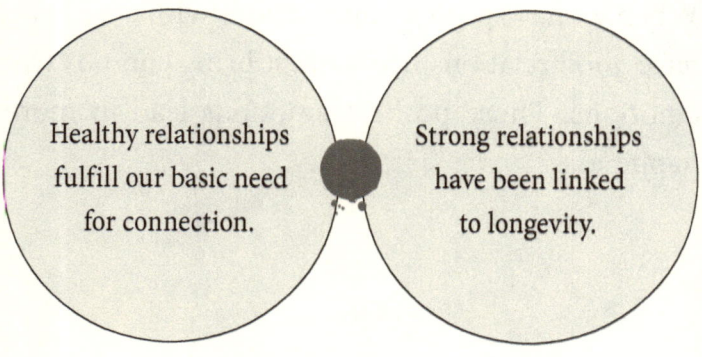

Healthy relationships fulfill our basic need for connection.

Strong relationships have been linked to longevity.

JULIE FIDALGO

Who are the people closest to you, and are those relationships positive or negative?

*"Choose your RELATIONSHIPS wisely.
It's better to be alone than
to be in bad company."*

-RUMI

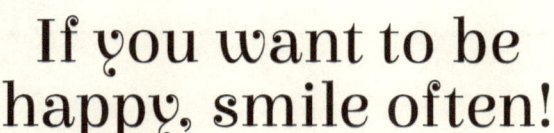

If you want to be happy, smile often!

Smiling can *actually* make you feel better and can even make you feel happy or joyful. Smiling releases endorphins, which leads to us feeling good!

Smiling also boosts your immune system, lowers blood pressure, and helps you relax. People who smile tend to live longer.

Studies have shown that people are attracted to those who smile. Smiling makes you more approachable and trustworthy. And when you smile, the people around you tend to smile as well.

How to smile often:

Practice smiling in the mirror and try to smile more often during the day.

Think happy thoughts and remind yourself of the things you're grateful for throughout the day. This will help you smile more often and make your smile more authentic.

Don't be afraid to show your teeth. The warmth of your smile is what's important.

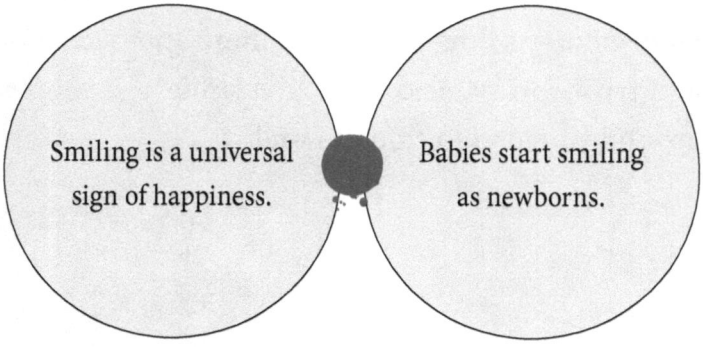

Smiling is a universal sign of happiness.

Babies start smiling as newborns.

What are some things that make you smile?

_____

_____

_____

_____

_____

_____

_____

_____

_____

_____

_____

_____

_____

_____

_____

_____

_____

_____

"Keep smiling, because life is a beautiful thing, and there's so much to SMILE about."

-MARILYN MONROE

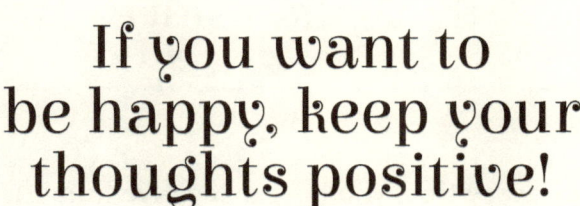

If you want to be happy, keep your thoughts positive!

Every thought has a frequency, which means thoughts vibrate in the mind. Positive thoughts such as love, joy, and gratitude create high frequency vibrations.

When we focus on positive thoughts and positive feelings, we attract more positive experiences and outcomes.

Choose your thoughts carefully. Thoughts control our feelings, and our thoughts and feelings create our life.

How to keep your thoughts positive:

Notice every time you have a negative thought and reframe it to a positive one. This may seem hard at first, but it gets easier with practice.

Don't believe all of your negative thoughts.

Focus on what you *do* have and be grateful for that!

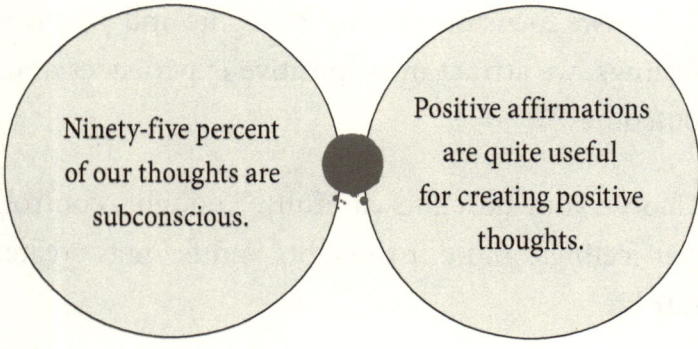

Ninety-five percent of our thoughts are subconscious.

Positive affirmations are quite useful for creating positive thoughts.

Write down all your negative
thoughts and then change
them to a positive one.

Ex: I can't do it → I CAN do it

_____

_____

_____

_____

_____

_____

_____

_____

_____

_____

_____

_____

_____

"Watch your THOUGHTS, they become your words; watch your words, they become your actions; watch your actions, they become your habits; watch your habits, they become your character; watch your character, it becomes your destiny."

-LAO TZU

If you want to be happy, be unique!

There are over eight billion people on earth. Imagine if we were all the same? Thankfully, we are all unique in our own special way. Embrace what makes you different.

We are happiest when we are true to ourselves and that means being authentic. It takes a lot of courage to be authentic and be your unique self.

Being unique is what makes you special. Trying to be someone else is not only a disservice to yourself but also a disservice to the world. When you learn to be happy with who you are and accept who you are, the sky is the limit!

How to be unique:

Have the courage and confidence to show up as your true self every day.

Remember that what makes you different is what makes you unique, which is what makes you stand out from the crowd. Don't be like everyone else.

Be truthful (with yourself and others), and always listen to your gut.

Identical twins may look the same, but they are still unique. They each have their own distinctive personality.

People often use the expression "follow your gut" when they talk about using your intuition.

What makes you unique?

_____

_____

_____

_____

_____

_____

_____

_____

_____

_____

_____

_____

_____

_____

_____

_____

_____

"Be yourself; everyone else is already taken. You are UNIQUE— just like everyone else."

-UNKNOWN

If you want to be happy, visualize!

Everything begins in the mind. Visualization is a technique used to program your subconscious mind by using images of what you desire and experiencing the feelings of already having it.

When you want something badly, start by visualizing it. The more real you can make it in your mind, the more powerful it is.

When you can see the vision in your mind, you can bring it to life. Having a vision of your future life is very important for a happy life.

How to visualize:

Sit somewhere quiet and get comfortable. Look for an object in the room and stare at it. Then close your eyes and try to see the object in your mind's eye.

Now try visualizing things you desire.

Create a vision board*. Hang it up where you can see it every day, and focus on it while experiencing the feelings of already having it.

Visualization can help the mind and body relax and reduce feelings of stress.

Visualization allows you to simulate the experience of having what you want in the present moment.

Describe in detail what you want to visualize into reality.

_____

_____

_____

_____

_____

_____

_____

_____

_____

_____

_____

_____

_____

_____

_____

_____

_____

"VISUALIZATION is the human being's vehicle to the future—good, bad, or indifferent. It's strictly in our control."

-EARL NIGHTINGALE

If you want to be happy, know your why!

Finding out what we like and don't like is easy. But we often miss the deeper question: WHY do I like doing this? What motivates me to like this?

It is important to answer this question because your why is your purpose. When we do things with purpose, we can achieve great things. This can bring greater fulfillment and make a positive impact on the world.

Our purpose guides us and keeps us on track. It keeps us committed to our goals and therefore passionate about reaching them. It keeps us focused on the end results.

How to find your why:

Ask yourself questions and explore what you want your ideal future to look like, keeping your interests and passions in mind.

Consider giving back or being of service to others.

Be kind and patient with yourself. You will find your why when the time is right.

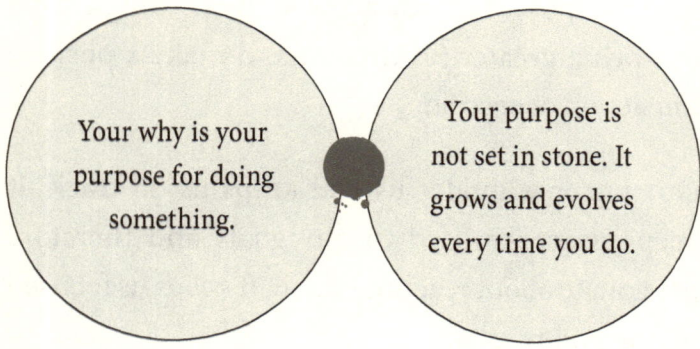

Your why is your purpose for doing something.

Your purpose is not set in stone. It grows and evolves every time you do.

What motivates you?

_____

_____

_____

_____

_____

_____

_____

_____

_____

_____

_____

_____

_____

_____

_____

_____

"When your WHY is big enough, you will find your how."

-LES BROWN

If you want to be happy, find your X-Factor!

Every single one of us is really good at something. There is a genius inside of you, and when you discover your X-Factor, that genius comes out.

There is something that you love to do that brings you incredible joy. Find that thing and develop it. The more you do what you love, the more joy it will bring you and everyone around you.

Some X-Factors are often not noticed, like being a good listener or being a good problem solver. Share your X-Factor with the world, and the world will thank you.

How to find your X-Factor:

Make a list of all the things you are good at, but at the same time, try new things.

Ask your family and friends what they think you are good at.

Keep practicing what you love and what you do well. This will bring you happiness.

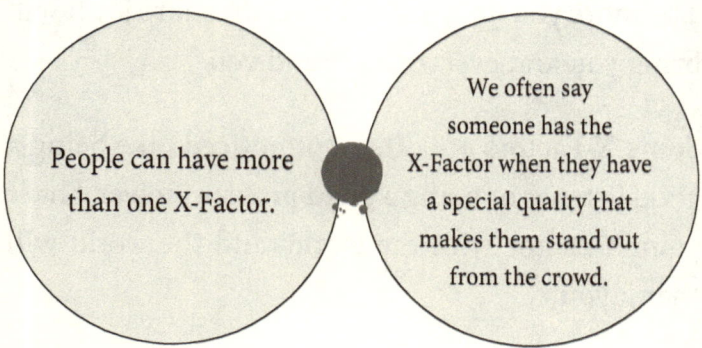

People can have more than one X-Factor.

We often say someone has the X-Factor when they have a special quality that makes them stand out from the crowd.

JULIE FIDALGO

Make a list of all of the things you are good at.

_____

_____

_____

_____

_____

_____

_____

_____

_____

_____

_____

_____

_____

_____

_____

*"Everyone has an X-FACTOR.
Find it, develop it, and
share it with the world."*

-JULIE FIDALGO

If you want to be happy, be you!

Happiness starts with you. The first step is to know who you are, what you stand for, and what you want your life to be like. Believe in yourself, and that will give you confidence.

Always remember that there is only one you. Embrace who you are and be kind to yourself. You are special, and you are here on earth for a reason.

You are only as important as you make yourself feel. Take good care of yourself. The only opinion that matters is yours. Make sure you think and feel good about yourself. Think *for* yourself, and remember that what *you* think about yourself is the most important opinion.

How to be you:

Get to know yourself; the good and the bad. Focus on the good parts of you.

Be proud of the things that make you different from other people.

Surround yourself with people who love you and accept you for who you are.

The chances of you being born are one in four hundred trillion.

You might think you know a lot about yourself, but you are always growing and changing. The quest for knowing yourself never stops.

JULIE FIDALGO

Who are you? Be honest with yourself.

_____

_____

_____

_____

_____

_____

_____

_____

_____

_____

_____

_____

_____

_____

_____

_____

_____

"YOU are the author of your life. If YOU don't like how it goes, write it differently."

-IVA KENAZ

If you want to be happy, have zest for life!

Zest is having enthusiasm and good energy. Happiness is about being passionate about life! It is when you get excited about doing things. In order to be happy, have zest for life.

Happy people have zest in everything they do. They are enthusiastic and do everything with positive energy.

If you look at life with zest, the little things that don't matter tend to go away. Look forward to new challenges with zest; every challenge then becomes an opportunity to embrace.

How to have more zest for life:

Approach every day with excitement and positive energy.

Discover what makes you happy and do more of that every day.

Be grateful for the things you have in life and get excited about the little stuff.

Studies suggest people with high levels of zest have better mental and physical health.

People can feel passion and good energy from others. Be the person people like to be around.

What are you passionate about, and how do you feel when you are doing that one thing?

_____

_____

_____

_____

_____

_____

_____

_____

_____

_____

_____

_____

_____

_____

*"If you have ZEST and enthusiasm,
you attract ZEST and enthusiasm.
Life does give back in kind."*

-NORMAN VINCENT PEALE

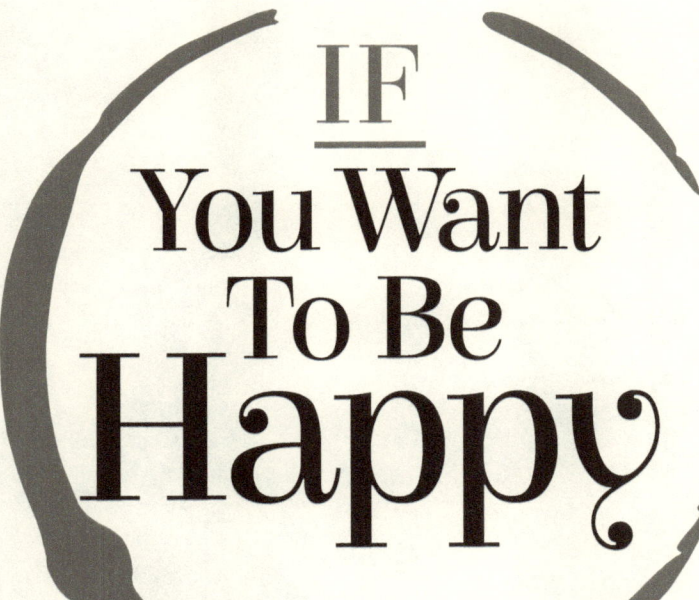

IF
You Want
To Be
Happy

A Final Word from Julie Fidalgo

Thank you for choosing this book out of the millions of books available and reading it to the end.

When I started on this journey, my intention was to write a short "self-improvement" book that was both straight to the point and easy to read, and this is why I wrote *If You Want to Be Happy*.

I realize most of the concepts written about in this book are simple, but they are often overlooked and are incredibly powerful. YOU are powerful! You can achieve anything *you* believe in.

Yes, there may be days or moments when you feel sad, angry, guilty, frustrated, hopeless, and/or disappointed; that just means you are human.

Life is a journey, and it's important that we continue to learn, grow, and believe.

My hope is for you to create your own happiness, even with all the challenges life throws at us.

I am dedicated to your happiness. Are you?

JULIE FIDALGO

"Life is 10% what happens to you and 90% how you react to it."

-CHARLES R. SWINDOLL

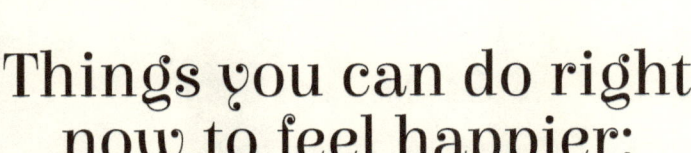

Things you can do right now to feel happier:

- ❖ Be in nature
- ❖ Take a walk
- ❖ Pet your dog/cat
- ❖ Dance!
- ❖ Laugh
- ❖ Meditate
- ❖ Call a friend
- ❖ Read a book
- ❖ Take a bubble bath
- ❖ Watch a funny movie
- ❖ Do puzzles
- ❖ Bake
- ❖ Go for a swim
- ❖ Plan a holiday
- ❖ Get a massage

- ❖ Listen to upbeat music
- ❖ Enjoy a cup of coffee
- ❖ Do some gardening
- ❖ Visit a Farmer's Market
- ❖ Eat ice cream (in moderation!)
- ❖ Take a class
- ❖ Go on a road trip
- ❖ Have a picnic
- ❖ Go camping
- ❖ Volunteer
- ❖ Learn something new
- ❖ Smell some flowers
- ❖ Cuddle with someone or a pet
- ❖ Get a manicure
- ❖ Do the thing you loved doing as a child
- ❖ Disconnect from technology
- ❖ Exercise (even if you don't feel like it!)
- ❖ Spend time with those you love
- ❖ Do something kind for a stranger
- ❖ Get some sun (vitamin D is good for you!)

Get creative!

JULIE FIDALGO

References

*Vision Board: A vision board, also known as a dream board, is a collage of images and/or words and affirmations used to inspire and motivate. It is used to remind yourself and your subconscious of what you desire.

*Meditation: A practice used to increase awareness, mindfulness, and a calm state.

Acknowledgments

To my mom and dad—I've always told you that the world would be a much better place if everyone had parents like you, and now I get to tell everyone! Thank you for instilling in me the idea and confidence that I can do anything. With persistence, passion, and faith, everything is possible. And I'm just getting started.

Mom, thank you for inspiring me with your strength, optimism, and discipline. Thank you for being authentic, loving, and supporting me unconditionally. You are so beautiful, inside and out. I admire everything about you, and when I grow up, I want to be just like you!

Dad, even though you are no longer with us, I wouldn't be where I am without you and your endless love, support, and encouragement. You always believed in me, and the continuous support had a resonating impact on my life. Thank you for being such a loving, generous, and noble human being and a great example of what a man and father ought to be.

To my sister, Lisiane—I am extremely grateful to have you in my life as someone I can talk to, trust, and count on to always be there for me.

André and Ariana—thank you for being you! Your authenticity and kindness inspire me every day to be better. I am so proud to be your aunt, and I know that this world is a better place with you in it. Always follow your heart and believe in yourself!

To the love of my life, Amer—words cannot describe how grateful I am to have you as my life partner. I admire you so much, and I thank you for your love, kindness, and loyalty. You mean the world to me. I love you.

To my cousin Paula—I feel so lucky to have you as my cousin. Thank you for your endless love.

To my dear friends—Maria Copello, Marcela Simões, Jessica Kuljis, Valentine Roche, Guia Reyes,

Claudia Briggs, Sara AlAjroush, Bia Antunes, Amel Malki, Chris Yen, and Sacha Awwa—no matter the time and/or distance, you have all contributed to my life in such a positive way. I love you all, and thank you for loving me for me!

To my favorite kids: Lara P., Caio P., Amalia W., Theo W., Charlie W., Maya D., Luna D., Maya R., Adam M., Dani M., Bella M. —You inspire me to be better, to do better, and to leave the world a better place. Thank you for being kind, loving, and happy human beings. I know for sure that the world is a better place with you in it. And remember, you can be, do, or have anything you want; you just need to believe you can and never give up. Always dream big!

To those who helped me with my book: Marni MacRae, Bryony van der Merwe, Jon Lasser, Sai Kumar, and Sara Husseini—I appreciate the patience and kindness you had with me as we worked to make this book what it is. Thank you.

To all the people along the way, including Tami Erickson and Lila Hattaway, who supported me one way or another—thank you!

To my best friend/sister Jessica Stadecker—It's hard to believe you are no longer with us on this earth, but your existence had a lifelong impact on me. You will forever live in my heart. Thank you for always being my #1 fan!

Thank you to the ones who purchased my book—I will forever be grateful to you.

Last but not least, I would like to thank God for all the blessings in my life.

About the Author

Julie Fidalgo has a dream; she wishes people would smile a little more often, feel a little more joy, and be a little more grateful. She dreams of inspiring happiness in a happier world. Just like you, Julie is quite familiar with  unpleasant life events; after all, life is filled with positive life experiences and negative ones. Through it all, she has always been able to find the silver lining in each situation, maintain a positive mindset, and create her happy.

Julie's experiences led her to write this book and share the simple concepts which have helped her throughout the years.

Julie received her B.A in Media Studies with a minor in Marketing, Advertising, and PR from Emerson College in Boston, MA. She went on to work in the entertainment industry in Los Angeles and then owned and operated a gourmet food truck. She is a life coach/ entrepreneur and believes this chapter of her life is the most important one yet.

She enjoys traveling, dancing, laughing, photography, nature, being with her family, and snuggling with her dog Rocky.

Julie is dedicated to your happiness. Are you?